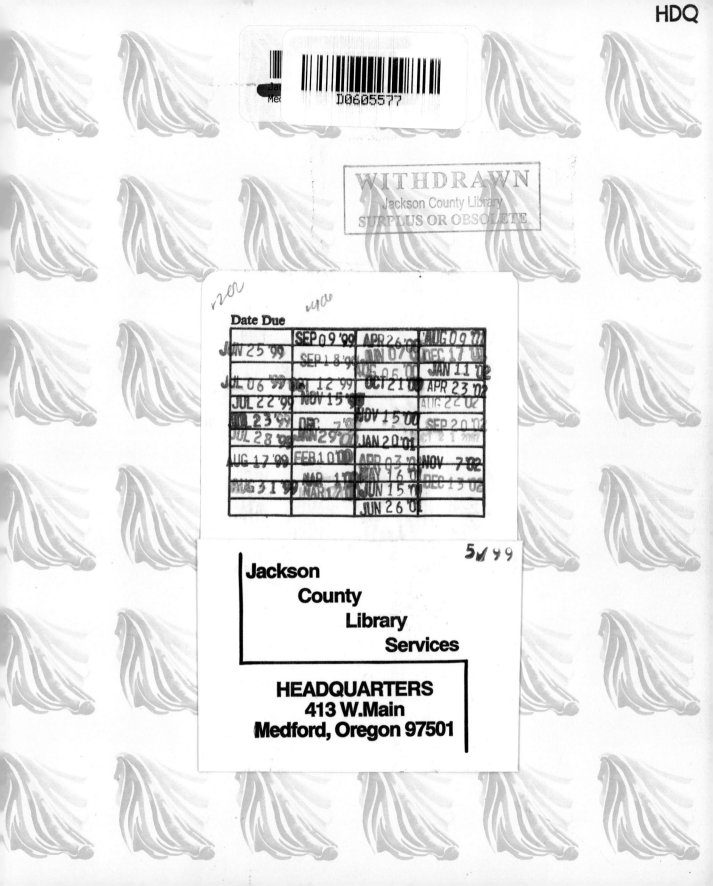

ínspirations

WINDOW TREATMENTS

Over 20 practical projects for curtains and blinds

inspirations

WINDOW TREATMENTS

Over 20 practical projects for curtains and blinds

ALISON JENKINS

PHOTOGRAPHY BY TIM IMRIE

LORENZ BOOKS

First published in 1998 by Lorenz Books

Lorenz Books is an imprint of
Anness Publishing Limited
Hermes House
88-89 Blackfriars Road
London SE1 8HA

This edition published in the USA by Lorenz Books
Anness Publishing Inc., 27 West 20th Street, New York, NY 10011
(800) 354-9657

A CIP catalogue record for this book is available from the British Library

ISBN 1-85967-750-9

Publisher: Joanna Lorenz
Senior Editor: Alison Macfarlane
Project Editor: Margaret Malone
Photography: Tim Imrie
Step photography: Rodney Forte
Stylist: Fanny Ward
Designer: Lilian Lindblom
Illustrators: Madeleine David and Lucinda Ganderton

Printed in Hong Kong/China

1 3 5 7 9 10 8 6 4 2

MEASUREMENTS
Both imperial and metric measurements have been given in the text. Where conversions produce an
awkward number, these have been rounded for convenience, but will produce an accurate result if one
system is used throughout.

CONTENTS

INTRODUCTION

In this book we will help you to transform your windows, and thereby an entire room, through clever and creative use of curtains and blinds. Much more than just something simply to hang at windows to keep the warmth in and the light out, curtains and blinds can be an essential part of a room's decorating scheme, making even the simplest window a point of interest in a plain room.

The projects in this book show how fabrics of different weight, texture, thickness and colour and simple additions, such as a row of coloured beads or buttons, can dramatically alter the way a window looks. Unbleached muslin allows a soft, diffused light into a room, while rows of tiny glass beads glitter in the sunshine. You can even change the shape of a window through your choice of curtain treatment: adding a pelmet to make a window seem taller, or making an extra wide window look more intimate by draping sheer voile curtains around the frame.

The starting point to all these projects is calculating how much fabric is required and cutting it out correctly. A detailed section at the back of this book shows you clearly and simply how to measure up a window, how to determine the necessary length and width of your fabric, and how to cut out plain and patterned fabrics. The section on basic techniques provides all the essential information you will need on how to use different pleats, headings, seams and hems to give each project an individual feel.

Each of the twenty two projects have been specially designed to be quick and easy to do. Expert sewing knowledge is not needed, as the detailed step-by-step instructions guide you through every stage. So whether you want to revamp an entire room or simply make better use of a window, this is the ideal book for every home-lover.

Deborah Barker

BASIC LINED CURTAINS

These easy steps show how simple it can be to make your own lined curtains.
A plain or striped fabric with a firm weave is the easiest to manage for your first attempt.
Detailed instructions for measuring up are at the back of the book.

YOU WILL NEED
scissors
tape measure
curtain fabric to fit window
lining fabric
pins
tailor's chalk (optional)
tacking thread
needle
sewing machine
matching thread
iron
pencil pleat curtain tape

1 Cut the curtain fabric to length, allowing a 2cm/¾in seam allowance at the top and 10cm/4in at the bottom of the curtain. Trim the lining fabric so that it is 4cm/1½in narrower and 7.5cm/3in shorter than the curtain fabric. Mark the centre top of each piece with a pin or tailor's chalk.

2 Fold, pin and tack a 2.5cm/1in double hem across the lower edge of the lining.

3 With right sides together, position the top of the lining 2cm/¾in down from the top edge of the curtain fabric. Pin the lining to the curtain down each side, keeping the edges even.

4 Machine-stitch down each side with a 2cm/¾in seam allowance. Stop stitching about 15cm/6in from the lower edge of the curtain.

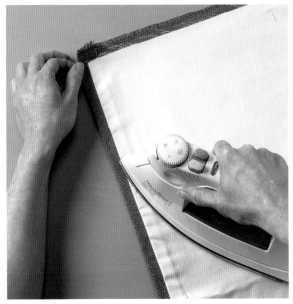

5 Turn the curtain through to the right side. Pin the fabric and lining together at the centre marks on the top edge, then press the side edges.

6 Turn up and press a 10cm/4in hem along the lower edge. Unfold the hem again and fold in the corners diagonally to meet the pressed line and create a mitred corner.

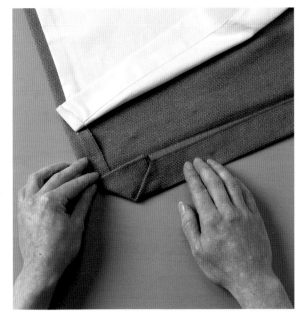

7 Fold in and press 5cm/2in of the hem allowance to enclose the raw edge.

8 Fold up the hem again and pin. Tack and stitch the hem invisibly along the folded edge. ▶

9 Turn the lining down over the hem and slip-stitch the remaining edge to the curtain.

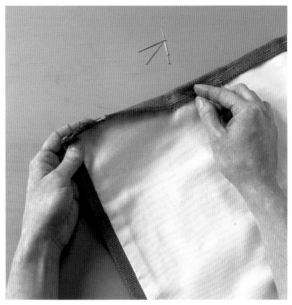

10 At the top of the curtain, fold the raw edge of the fabric over the lining and pin in place.

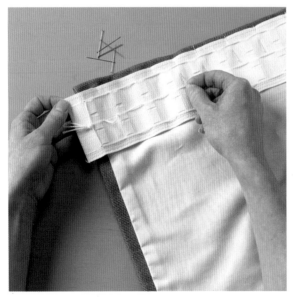

11 Pull out the cords of the curtain tape for a few centimetres and tie together in a secure knot. Trim the tape about 2cm/¾in from the knot. Position the curtain tape about 5mm/¼in from the upper edge and pin.

12 Tuck in the raw edge at each end of the curtain tape, then machine-stitch along the guide lines on both edges of the tape. Stitch in the same direction each time to avoid puckering.

APPLIQUED GINGHAM DAISIES

Though charmingly rustic and fresh looking, black-and-white gingham makes a smart,
crisp trimming for a neutral linen curtain. Arrange the flowers at varying heights
to give the impression that they are growing up from the hem.

YOU WILL NEED
tape measure
scissors
plain linen fabric
iron
sewing machine
matching thread
gingham
needle
pins
tracing paper
pencil
fusible bonding web
small amounts of plain and gingham fabrics

1 Measure the width of the curtain pole and decide on the length of the curtain. Cut the fabric to one and a half times the width and add 10cm/4in to the length for seam allowances. Turn in and press a 1cm/½in double hem down both side edges and a 5cm/2in double hem along the bottom edge. Machine-stitch all three hems.

2 Calculate the number of ties needed, spacing them about 20cm/8in apart. For each tie, cut a piece of gingham 6 x 40cm (2½ x 16in). Fold in half lengthways, right sides together. Stitch along the length, press the seam to the centre and stitch across one end. Trim and turn through. Tuck in the raw edges and slip-stitch the remaining end.

3 Turn over and press to the right side a 1cm/½in single hem at the top of the curtain. Fold the ties in half widthways and pin the folded ends to the top edge of the curtain on the right side, spacing them evenly. Machine-stitch in place.

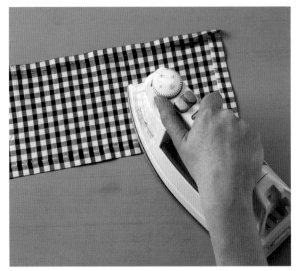

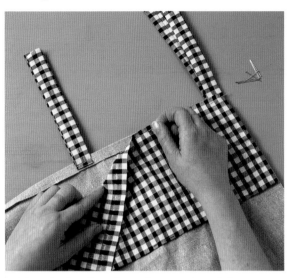

4 To make the heading, cut a 14cm/5½in strip of gingham to the width of the curtain plus 4cm/1½in. Fold and press a 2cm/¾in turning on all sides of the strip.

5 Lay the heading along the top edge of the curtain, matching the folded edges, and pin in position. Machine-stitch all round the heading.

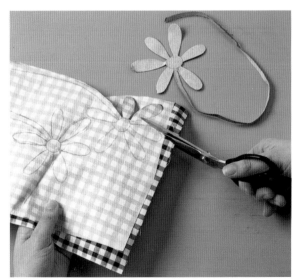

6 Scale up the daisy template at the back of the book. Trace as many flower shapes as you will need on to a piece of fusible bonding web and cut out roughly. Lay the shapes sticky side down on a selection of plain and gingham fabrics. Press to fuse them in place. Cut the motifs out carefully.

7 Peel away the paper backing and arrange the flower motifs across the hem of the curtain. When you are happy with the design, press to fuse them in place.

▶

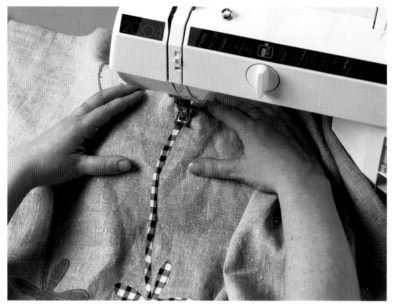

8 Machine-stitch around each flower motif, using straight stitch, keeping as close to the edge of the motif as possible.

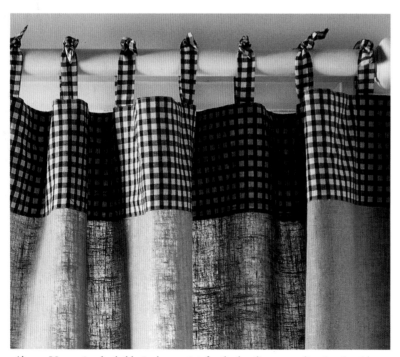

Above: Use a simple, bold gingham print for the heading, co-ordinating it with cushions and table settings for a pretty overall effect.

SWAGGED KITCHEN SHELF

This informal, scaled-down version of traditional swags and tails takes the place of curtains and is just right for a kitchen window, particularly as the pelmet board from which it hangs is wide enough to make a useful shelf.

YOU WILL NEED
23 x 2.5cm/9 x 1in milled
timber, 40cm/16in wider than
the window
sandpaper
tape measure
2 metal brackets, 20 x 25cm/
8 x 10in
pencil
drill
six 1cm/½in No 8 screws
screwdriver
2.5cm/1in wide ribbon

scissors
staple gun
spirit level
6 wall plugs
six 4cm/1½in No 8 screws
120cm/48in wide fabric
ruler or set square
pins
sewing machine
matching thread
needle
iron

1 Smooth the sawn edges of the timber with sandpaper.

2 Position the brackets 10cm/4in from each end of the shelf. The shorter arm of the bracket should be positioned so that the longer arm will lie against the wall. Mark the positions of the screw-holes on the wood in pencil.

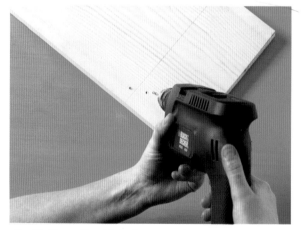

3 Drill small guideholes 5mm/¼in deep. Using the 1cm/½in screws, screw the brackets to the wood.

4 Cut four 15cm/6in lengths of ribbon and attach one to each corner of the underside of the shelf using a staple gun. Turn the raw edges under and secure with a staple.

5 Using a spirit level, position the shelf over the window so that there is an overhang either side of 20cm/8in. Mark the positions for the screw-holes on the wall. Drill holes 2.5cm/1in deep and place a wall plug in each hole. Attach the shelf to the wall using the 4cm/1½in screws.

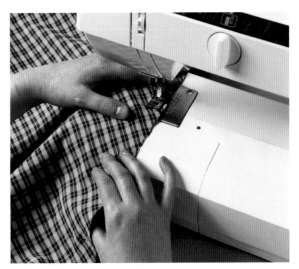

6 Decide on the length of the "tails" beside the window. You will need a piece of fabric about four times this length. Fold it in half lengthways and cut it out following the diagram at the back of the book.

7 With right sides together and a 2cm/¾in seam allowance, stitch around the cut edges, leaving a 15cm/6in gap in the stitching. Clip away the seam allowance at the corners.

▶

8 Pull the fabric through the gap in the seam to the right side.

9 Invisibly slip-stitch the gap in the seam by hand to close.

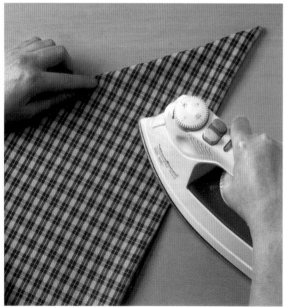

10 Press the seams flat to achieve a crisp, straight finish to the curtain tail.

11 Thread the fabric through the ribbon loops under the front of the shelf and arrange in a swag. Pull the tails through the loops at the back.

CUT-OUT DENIM ROLLER BLIND

The roller blind makes a classically neat, unfussy window treatment. This project uses a roller blind kit, but it can be just as effective to buy a ready-made blind and give it extra dash by adding a pattern of peep-holes across the fabric, as shown here.

YOU WILL NEED

roller blind kit	tailor's chalk
saw	pins
screwdriver	tear-away backing fabric
tape measure	small, sharp scissors
scissors	iron
denim fabric	wooden lath
sewing machine	fabric stiffener spray
matching thread	tacks
stiff card	hammer
	wooden acorn or large bead

1 Cut the roller to fit the window and fix the brackets and roller in place. Measure the width of the roller and the length of the window. Cut the fabric to this size, adding 30cm/12in to the length. Work a zig-zag stitch along the side edges.

2 Cut a small rectangular template from a piece of card. Using tailor's chalk, draw around the template at even intervals across the blind.

3 Pin a piece of tear-away backing fabric under each rectangular shape. Work a straight stitch around the edge.

4 Using small, sharp scissors, carefully cut away the fabric from inside the rectangle.

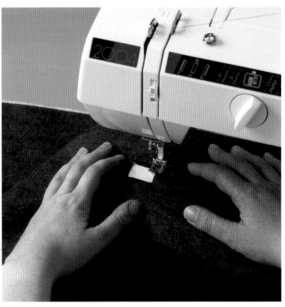

5 Work a satin stitch enclosing the raw edges. Tear away the backing fabric.

6 Turn and press to the wrong side a double hem of 4cm/1½in. Machine-stitch the hem. Cut the lath 4cm/1½in shorter than the width of the blind and insert it into the casing.

7 Machine-stitch across each end of the casing, enclosing the lath.

▶

8 Hang the fabric in a well-ventilated room. Spray the fabric with the stiffener, following the manufacturer's instructions. Leave to dry.

9 Lay the fabric face up and place the roller across it with the adhesive strip face up, 4cm/1½in from the top edge. Pull the edge of the fabric over and press it firmly to the adhesive strip.

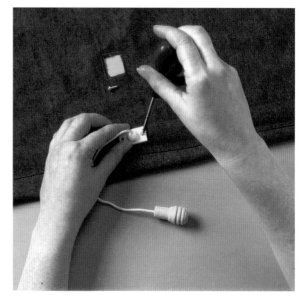

10 Hammer tacks in place at 2cm/¾in intervals along the roller, placing one at each end. Roll up the blind.

11 Thread a wooden acorn or a large bead on to the cord supplied. Screw the cord to the centre of the lath.

KITCHEN PRINT CURTAINS

*These kitchen curtains, smothered with pictures of lavish Victorian desserts, have been
decorated using transfer cream, which will duplicate any photocopied image on to fabric.
Old books of engravings are a mine of appropriate prints.*

YOU WILL NEED
tape measure
scissors
white cotton fabric
photocopier
black and white images
image transfer cream
paintbrush
sponge
iron
pins
sewing machine
matching thread
2.5cm/1in wide white cotton tape

1 Measure the window and decide on the finished
length of the curtains. Cut the fabric to size,
adding a 2cm/¾in seam allowance all round each
curtain. Photocopy your chosen images in black and
white. Cut out close to the edge of each image.

2 Read the manufacturer's instructions on the
transfer cream before you begin. Paint the cream
over the photocopies.

24

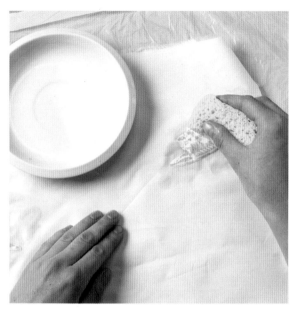

3 Place each photocopy face down on the fabric and smooth out the paper to remove any air bubbles. Apply the images all over the fabric and leave to dry for a minimum of 4 hours.

4 At the end of the drying period, dab a wet sponge over each photocopied image to moisten the paper.

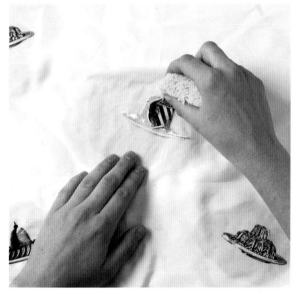

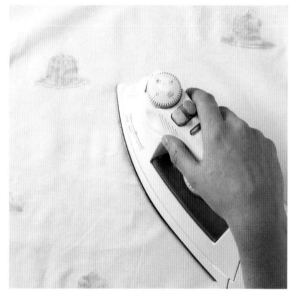

5 Gently rub off the paper with the damp sponge and the tips of your fingers.

6 When all the paper has been removed and the fabric is dry, iron the fabric on the wrong side to fix the images.

▶

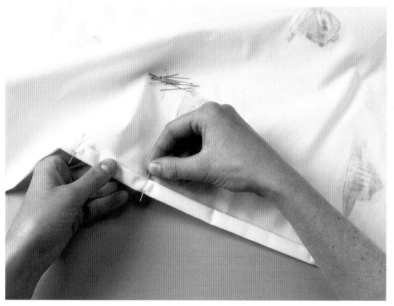

7 Pin under a 1cm/½in double hem all round each curtain. Machine-stitch in place.

8 Cut 75cm/30in lengths of white cotton tape and fold them in half. Pin the folded edge of each piece of tape to the top of the curtain, spacing them evenly about 20cm/8in apart. Machine-stitch in place. Tie the tapes in bows to the curtain pole.

DRAPED MUSLIN CURTAINS

A swagged and draped design enhances a beautifully proportioned window, but the curtains need not be heavy. Billowing muslin makes the lightest of window dressings, while retaining all the elegance of traditional full-length curtains.

YOU WILL NEED
tape measure
scissors
muslin
pins
iron
sewing machine
matching thread
paper
pencil
ruler
bobble trim

1 Measure the length from the pole to the floor and add 30cm/12in. The width of the curtains will depend on how much fullness you want. Cut two curtains to size. Turn in, press and machine-stitch a 1cm/½in double hem along all sides.

2 For the central draped section, make a paper pattern in the shape of a trapezium. The top edge should be the desired width between the curtains plus 40cm/16in. The bottom edge should be the width of both curtains plus 50cm/20in. The height should be the width of one curtain plus 30cm/12in.

3 Cut the fabric to size and press a 1cm/½in double hem along the top and bottom edges. Machine-stitch. Run a gathering stitch along the raw side edges.

▶

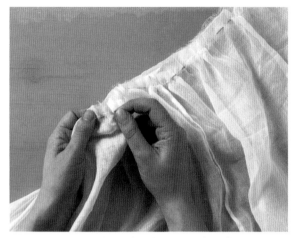

4 Pin the top edge of each curtain length to one gathered side edge of the central panel, with the wrong side of the curtain to the right side of the panel. Distribute the gathers evenly and stitch.

5 Cut two strips of muslin the width of the pole circumference plus 2cm/¾in seam allowance. Fold in half lengthways and press. Stitch one long side to the right side of the top edge of each curtain, then fold over and pin and stitch the other side, turning in the seam allowance and enclosing the raw edges.

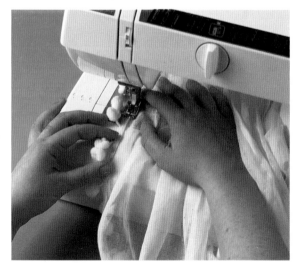

6 Cut two pieces of bobble trim the length of the curtains plus 4cm/1½in. Pin the trim to the inner edges of the curtains, turning in the raw ends. Machine-stitch. Cut a piece of bobble trim to fit the bottom edge of the draped section plus 4cm/1½in. Pin to the edge and machine-stitch.

7 Thread the pole through the casings. Fold the draped section over the pole to the front.

RIBBON CAFE CURTAIN

To dress up a small window, create this luxurious striped curtain using ribbons instead of fabric. Rows of tiny glass beads add extra sparkle to the satin; larger beads make a pretty hem and add weight to hold the ribbons straight.

YOU WILL NEED
scissors
2.5cm/1in wide satin and chiffon ribbons in toning colours
sugar
small bowl
sewing machine
matching thread
tacking thread
needle
small glass beads
large faceted plastic beads
tension rod or curtain wire to fit across window

1 Cut the ribbons to the finished length of the curtain plus 4cm/1½in. Trim one end of each ribbon length into decorative points.

2 Dissolve some sugar in a little water in a small bowl. To prevent the raw ends of the ribbon from fraying, dip the trimmed ends of each length into the solution and leave to dry.

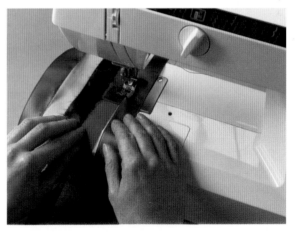

3 Lay out enough ribbons in a repeating pattern, alternating satin and chiffon, to fit the width of the window. Using matching thread and a small zig-zag stitch, join the ribbons together. End each seam 7.5cm/3in from the bottom. ▶

4 Fold over 5mm/¼in then another 2.5cm/1in along the top edge to make a casing and tack. Starting below the casing, hand-stitch small glass beads along each seam.

5 Thread a large plastic bead on to the end of each satin ribbon as shown. Machine-stitch the casing and thread the tension rod or curtain wire through it to hang the curtain.

STAMPED CALICO BLIND

Ready-made stamps are available in hundreds of different shapes: use them with fabric paints to create made-to-measure designs for curtains and blinds. Here, the cords are threaded through large eyelets that are decorative as well as functional.

YOU WILL NEED
tape measure
scissors
medium-weight calico
pins
fabric paints
plate
applicator sponges
high-density foam stamps
iron
sewing machine
matching thread
needle
pencil
eyelet kit
1.5cm/⅝in brass eyelets
nylon cord
2 spring toggles
9mm/⅜in wooden dowel
2 screw-in hooks

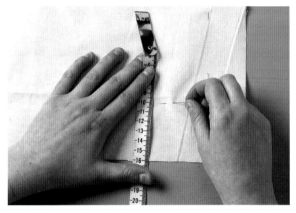

1 Measure the window to establish the finished size of the blind. Cut two pieces of calico, adding 4cm/1½in to the width and 7cm/2¾in to the length. On one piece, use pins to mark out the area for the stamped design, allowing 5cm/2in on either side for the eyelets, 3cm/1¼in at the top and 6cm/2½in at the bottom.

2 Squeeze out a small amount of each fabric paint on to a plate. Using an applicator sponge, apply an even coating of paint to the first stamp.

3 Stamp your design on to the calico, applying an even pressure. Apply fresh paint to the stamp for each motif to keep the colour consistent.

4 Complete the design and leave to dry. Iron the calico on the wrong side to fix the paint.

5 With right sides together, pin the printed calico to the plain piece of calico around all the edges.

6 With a 2cm/¾in seam allowance at the top and sides and a 5cm/2in allowance at the bottom, machine-stitch the edges. Leave a 15cm/6in gap on one side and a 2cm/¾in gap at the top of each side seam.

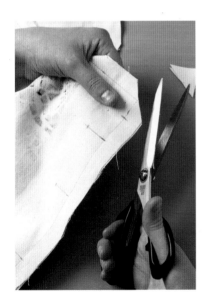

7 Clip the seam allowance at the corners.

8 Turn the blind right side out through the gap left in the side seam.

9 Press flat all the edges of the blind.

10 Slip-stitch the gap in the side seam by hand to close.

11 Mark the eyelet positions up each side of the blind about 7.5cm/3in apart. Insert the eyelets using a kit.

12 Thread a length of nylon cord through the eyelets on each side of the blind, knotting it at the top.

13 Thread the bottom end of each length of cord through a spring toggle.

14 Finish the cord at the bottom with a knot and trim off the excess.

15 Cut a length of dowel 4cm/1½in wider than the blind and thread it through the gaps in the top corners. Screw two hooks into the top corners of the window frame from which to hang the blind.

ORCHARD PRINT CURTAINS AND BLIND

The co-ordinating blind and curtains give a very finished look to this design, printed with real fruits, while the unbleached muslin casts a gentle, flattering light.

YOU WILL NEED

scissors	pear
unbleached muslin	fabric paints in red, green and
tape measure	black
unbleached calico	paintbrush
iron	thick card
pins	small plastic rings
sewing machine	9mm/³/₈in wooden dowel
matching thread	lengths cut to the width of the
tacking thread	finished blind
needle	nylon cord
tailor's chalk	staple gun
transparent net tape	wooden batten to fit window
kitchen knife	recess
apple	2 screw-in eyes
	pencil pleat curtain tape

1 To make the blind, cut a muslin panel to the same size as the window plus a 2cm/¾in seam allowance at each side and at the lower edge and 5cm/2in at the top. Cut calico strips 13cm/5in wide to fit the sides and the lower edge. To mitre at the lower corners, cut the lower ends of the side strips and both ends of the bottom strip at 45°.

2 Press and pin a 2cm/¾in hem to the wrong side along the inside edge of each calico border piece.

3 Pin and machine-stitch the mitres together then press the seams flat.

4 Pin and stitch the right side of the border to the wrong side of the muslin, with a 2cm/¾in seam. Trim the seam allowance and clip each corner.

5 Turn the border through to the right side and press. Pin, tack and machine top-stitch the border piece close to the fold.

6 Divide the blind into horizontal sections no more than 30cm/12in deep, making the bottom section about two-thirds the depth of the other sections. On the wrong side, pin and stitch transparent tape along each marked line to take the dowel.

7 Cut the apple and the pear in half. Using red paint on the apple and green on the pear, print around the fabric border. Recoat the fruit with paint after each print and press firmly.

8 Cut a small piece of thick card and bend it slightly. Dip the side of the card into a little black paint and print a stalk on each fruit. Allow to dry. ▶

9 Turn the blind over and stitch a small plastic ring to each end of the dowel channels, then insert the lengths of dowel.

10 Tie a length of cord to each ring of the lowest channel, then thread it through the other rings to the top. Use a staple gun to attach the blind to the batten. Position a screw-in eye in the batten over each line of rings and thread the cords through, taking both cords to one side of the blind.

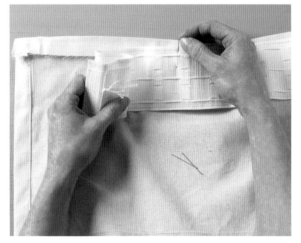

11 For the curtains, cut out the calico fabric to the length required plus 12.5cm/5in. Fold and stitch a double 2.5cm/1in hem down each side, then fold, pin and stitch a double 5cm/2in hem along the lower edge. Turn down 2.5cm/1in across the upper edge of each curtain. Cut the curtain tape about 4cm/1½in longer than the curtain width.

12 Draw out the cords and tie in a knot at each end. Pin the tape to the curtain about 5mm/¼in down from the upper edge. Tuck in the raw edges of the tape at each end. Stitch the tape in place along the guidelines on both edges. Using the apple and pear halves as before, print a random design all over the curtains.

RIBBON FLOWERS

Sheer curtains don't have to be white: choose a fabric in a vibrant shade and add an assortment of equally bright ribbons, coiled into flowers, to decorate your window with a riot of colour. A wider ribbon forms the casing at the top.

YOU WILL NEED
tape measure
scissors
sheer fabric
tailor's chalk
embroidery hoop
tacking thread
needle
9mm/³⁄₈in wide satin ribbons in assorted colours
sewing machine
matching threads
iron
self-cover buttons
scraps of coloured fabrics
easy button cover
4cm/1¹⁄₂in wide satin ribbon
pins

1 Measure the window and decide on the finished length of the curtain. Cut the fabric to length, adding 4cm/1½in for seam allowances. The fabric should be at least one and a half times the width of the window. Lay out the fabric on a flat surface and decide where you want to stitch the flowers. Mark each position with tailor's chalk. Fit an embroidery hoop over the first marked point.

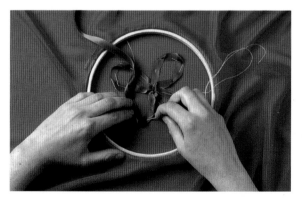

2 Tack a length of 9mm/³⁄₈in wide ribbon in the shape of a flower on to the fabric inside the embroidery hoop. Cut off the excess ribbon.

3 Machine-stitch the flower in place, then coil a length of contrasting ribbon in the centre and stitch. Make the other flowers in different coloured ribbons. ▶

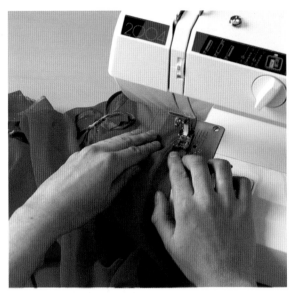

4 Fold and press 1cm/½in double hems all round the fabric. Machine-stitch.

5 Cover some self-cover buttons with scraps of fabric in assorted colours. Use an easy button cover to speed up the process.

6 Cut a piece of 4cm/1½in ribbon to the width of the curtain plus 2cm/¾in. Hand-stitch the buttons, evenly spaced, in a line along the centre.

7 Fold over the ends of the ribbon so that it fits the width of the curtain and pin it in place 1cm/½in below the top edge. Machine-stitch along each side of the ribbon to make a casing for the curtain wire.

VOILE STRIPES

Sheer, unstructured curtains in a mixture of brilliant colours have an ethnic feel.
Choose a colour for the backing panel that will enhance the mixture and increase its richness.
You can sew the sides or leave them hanging free as shown here.

YOU WILL NEED
tape measure
scissors
voile fabrics in three colours
tailor's chalk
pins
sewing machine
matching threads
iron
voile backing fabric
2.5cm/1in wide ribbon or braid
9mm/³⁄₈in satin ribbon

1 Measure the window and decide on the length of the curtains. Cut the voile fabrics into panels that will make a total width at least one and a half times that of the window. In each curtain, the two outside panels are the same width and the centre panel is slightly wider. Add 3cm/1¼in to the length for the seam allowances.

2 With right sides together, pin each centre panel to one of the side panels and machine-stitch with a 1cm/½in seam allowance. Sew on the other side panels. Press the seams open. Cut the backing fabric to the same size as the curtains.

3 Cut a length of 2.5cm/1in ribbon or braid for each joined seam and pin it over the seam. Machine-stitch in place down both edges.

▶

4 Fold over, press and machine-stitch a double 1cm/½in hem down each side of the curtains and along the lower edge. Repeat around the sides and lower edge of the backing fabric.

5 Cut some lengths of 9mm/⅜in satin ribbon, long enough to fit over the curtain pole, for the hanging loops. Fold the loops in half and pin the raw edges to the top edge of the curtains, spacing them evenly about 20cm/8in apart.

6 Pin the backing fabric to each curtain along the top edge, right sides together, and machine-stitch, trapping the ribbon loops. Turn the backing fabric to the back of the curtain and press the seam.

PLEATED TISSUE BLIND

Delicate handmade tissue paper makes a surprisingly sturdy blind. Two sheets are pasted together and the edges are doubled again for added strength. The paper folds crisply into pleats, and smart silky tassels complete the oriental look.

YOU WILL NEED
wallpaper paste
pasting brush
handmade tissue paper
tape measure
scissors
double-sided tape
ruler
pencil
eyelet tool and eyelets
thin coloured cord
2 small tassels to match cord
staple gun
wooden batten to fit window recess
2 screw-in eyes

1 Mix up the wallpaper paste following the manufacturer's instructions and paste together two sheets of tissue paper. Leave to dry. Measure the window recess, adding 5cm/2in to the width and 15cm/6in to the length. Cut the tissue to size. Apply double-sided tape to the sides and lower edge.

2 Remove the backing paper and fold a 2.5cm/1in hem down each side.

3 Apply double-sided tape to the lower edge of the blind then fold a 2.5cm/1in hem along its length.

4 On the back of the blind, mark horizontal lines with a ruler and pencil 5cm/2in apart.

5 Fold the blind into regular pleats along the marked lines.

6 Mark the centre of each side seam and the centre of each pleat. Use an eyelet tool to pierce a hole at the marked position on each fold.

7 Using the eyelet tool, insert the eyelets at each of the holes along the fold.

▶

8 Tie a tassel to the end of a length of cord and pass it through the eyelets. Repeat with a second length of cord on the other side.

9 Use a staple gun to attach the blind to the top of the wooden batten. Position the screw-in eyes at the back of the batten above the eyelet holes and pass the cord through them, threading one cord through both so that the two ends hang to one side of the blind.

RAINFOREST STENCIL

Both the positive and negative parts of this stencil are used to create a sophisticated pattern from a single, almost abstract motif. Light streaming through the unlined cotton enhances the hothouse look of this design.

YOU WILL NEED

scissors	pencil
lightweight plain cotton fabric	ruler
tape measure	acetate sheet
iron	masking tape
pins	cutting mat
sewing machine	craft knife
matching thread	tailor's chalk
needle	spray adhesive
buttons	large stencil brush
tracing paper	fabric paint

1 Cut the fabric to size for the curtains, allowing 5cm/2in seam allowances at the sides and lower edge and 2cm/¾in at the top. Fold, pin and machine-stitch 2.5cm/1in double hems down each side, then repeat the process for the hem at the bottom.

2 Calculate the number of tabs you will need, spacing them about 20cm/8in apart. Cut a rectangle of fabric for each tab, using the template at the back of the book. Fold each rectangle in half lengthways and stitch, with a 1cm/½in seam allowance. Open out the seam allowance and pin and stitch across one end of the tab so the seam lies at the centre.

3 Turn each tab to the right side and press. Pin the raw ends to the right side of each curtain, spacing the tabs evenly along the top. For the facing, cut a 7.5cm/3in strip of fabric the width of the curtain plus 4cm/1½in for seam allowances. Pin the strip to the curtain with right sides together and machine-stitch the top edge.

4 Fold the facing to the wrong side, fold in the seam allowances at each end and along the raw edge and pin in place.

5 Machine-stitch the facing close to the folded edge.

6 Fold the tabs over on to the front of the curtain and hand-stitch a button to hold each one in place.

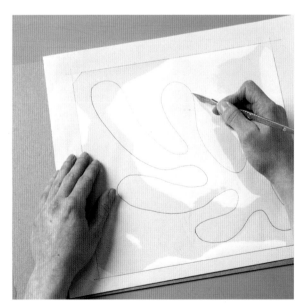

7 Scale up the stencil design from the back of the book. Cut a square of acetate the size of the design and fasten it to the paper with tabs of masking tape. Place the paper and acetate on a cutting mat and carefully cut out the design using a craft knife. Retain the cut-out part of the stencil for the negative images.

8 Using tailor's chalk, mark the curtains into squares the same size as the stencil. Use spray adhesive to fix the stencil in place in the first marked square. Using a large stencil brush apply fabric paint sparingly to the stencil to create a mottled effect. Leave the stencil in place.

▶

9 To make the negative image, mask off the areas around the square with masking tape.

10 Use spray adhesive to fix the cut-out motif in the centre, then apply fabric paint all round it. Remove the stencils and move to the next marked squares. Repeat all over the curtains. When the paint is dry, fix it with a hot iron following the manufacturer's instructions.

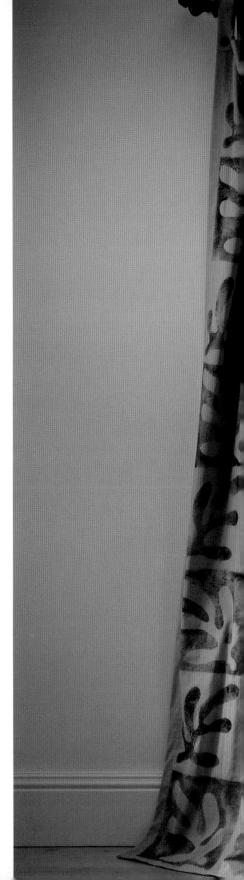

FALLING LEAVES

The autumn leaves tumbling down this translucent panel look as if they are falling from the trees outside. These are cut out of paper, but if you find some beautiful real leaves you could press them and put them in the pockets instead.

YOU WILL NEED
scissors
organza
tape measure
iron
pins
matching thread
sewing machine
tracing paper
pencil
coloured paper in several autumnal shades
small scissors
wooden batten to fit across window
staple gun

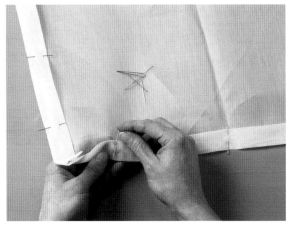

1 Cut a piece of organza to the size of the window plus 5cm/2in for hems all round. Turn in, press and pin 2.5cm/1in double hems down both sides and across the lower edge.

2 Use matching thread and a machine satin stitch to stitch over the fold of each hem.

3 Decide how many leaves you will have room for on your panel. Copy the leaf templates at the back of the book and trace on to coloured paper.

4 Cut out the paper leaves with a pair of small scissors.

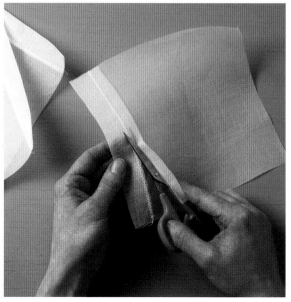

5 Cut organza pockets to fit the leaf shapes, allowing an extra 2.5cm/1in at the upper edge. Fold over the hem allowance, press and satin-stitch 2cm/¾in from the edge. Trim off the excess fabric.

6 Pin and satin-stitch the pockets in place on the panel. Insert a leaf in each pocket, alternating the colours to make a pleasing design.

7 Lay the wooden batten along the top of the blind, pull the fabric tightly around the batten and staple in place at the back.

SLATTED BROCADE BLIND

The luxurious textures and colours of brocade ribbons are irresistible when mixed together, and here is an ingenious way of adapting this richness to dress up a window. The opulent effect is completed with gold beads and silken cords.

YOU WILL NEED
tape measure
4cm/1½in wide stripwood
saw
sandpaper
4cm/1½in wide brocade ribbon in several toning patterns
scissors
craft glue
silk cord
adhesive tape
gold beads with large central holes
9mm/⅜in wooden dowel to fit window recess
matching thread

1 Divide the length of the window by 6cm/2½in to estimate the approximate number of wooden slats you will need. Cut the slats to the width of the window less 3cm/1¼in and sand the rough edges.

2 Cut lengths of brocade ribbon and glue to both sides of each slat.

3 Turn the raw edges under and glue neatly at each end.

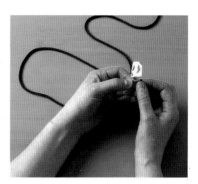

4 Cut two lengths of silk cord twice the length of the window plus 30cm/12in. Wind a piece of adhesive tape around each end to stop it fraying. ▶

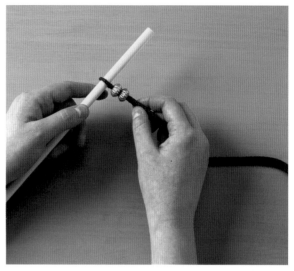

5 Double a length of cord and thread on two gold beads, pulling them up to make a loop.

6 Slot the wooden dowel through the loop and pull tight. Repeat with the other piece of cord and two more beads.

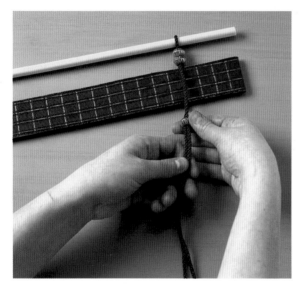

7 Thread another bead on to the doubled cord and pull up, encasing the end of a brocade-covered slat. Repeat with the other cord to encase the other end of the slat. Continue to thread beads on to each cord, securing the slats as you go.

8 At the foot of the blind, finish each cord with a single bead. Knot the cord and neaten the ends by wrapping a piece of adhesive tape around them under the knot. Trim away the excess and wind a piece of matching cotton thread around the tip to hide the tape.

DOUBLE FAN BLIND

Two narrow pleated blinds hung side by side and caught up in the middle take on a wonderfully precise and unusual shape at the window. The striped fabric accentuates the visual precision of the pleats and makes them easier to fold.

YOU WILL NEED
tape measure
scissors
stiffened muslin
fabric with 4cm/1½in wide horizontal stripes
iron
pins
tacking thread
needle
1cm/½in wide cotton tape
sewing machine
matching thread
2 large buttons
9mm/⅜in wooden dowel
2 screw-in hooks

1 Measure the window recess and cut a piece of stiffened muslin to the finished size of the blind, 7.5cm/3in longer than the window and half its width less 1cm/½in. Place the muslin on the wrong side of the striped fabric and cut around it, adding a 3cm/1¼in seam allowance all round. Cut a second piece of fabric, matching the stripes. Fold the seam allowance over the muslin and tack along each edge.

2 Fold in and press the seam allowance around the second piece of fabric. Place the edges together, sandwiching the muslin between the two layers of fabric. Pin and tack around the sides and the bottom.

3 Cut a 60cm/24in length of cotton tape. Fold it in half and tuck the raw ends into the centre of the top, untacked edge. Pin and tack along this edge.

▶

4 Top-stitch close to the folded edges all round the blind, leaving a 2cm/¾in gap in the stitching at the top of each side. Following the lines of the stripes, press in concertina pleats.

5 Sew a button in the top centre of the blind, 4cm/1½in down from the top edge. Repeat steps 1 to 5 to make a second, matching blind.

6 Thread a single length of wooden dowel through the gaps in the top corners of both blinds.

7 Draw up the blinds by hooking the cotton tape loops around the buttons. Screw a hook into each top corner of the window to hang the blinds.

WOVEN ORGANZA BLIND

Glamorous metallic organza lets the daylight through while obscuring the view from outside so this sparkling woven blind, with its delicate, watery sheen, would be particularly appropriate for an unfrosted bathroom window.

YOU WILL NEED
scissors
metallic organza in two different colours
tape measure
pins
tacking thread
needle
sewing machine
matching thread
9mm/³⁄₈in wooden dowel to fit across the window
2 screw-in hooks

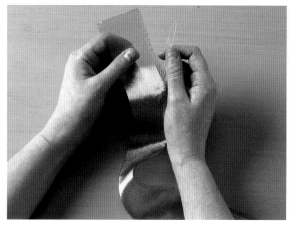

1 Cut the metallic organza into strips 5cm/2in wide, at right angles to the selvedge. The vertical strips, in one colour, should be at least 10cm/4in longer than the finished blind length, and the horizontal strips in the other colour should be about 4cm/1½in wider than the finished width. Fray the edges of all the strips.

2 On a large table, lay out the horizontal strips of organza.

3 Interweave the vertical and horizontal strips, pinning each intersection.

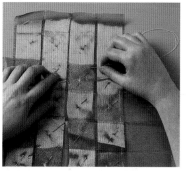

4 Leave 7.5cm/3in tabs along the top edge. When the required size has been reached tack all round the outer edge. ▶

5 Fold the tabs along the top edge over and tack in place.

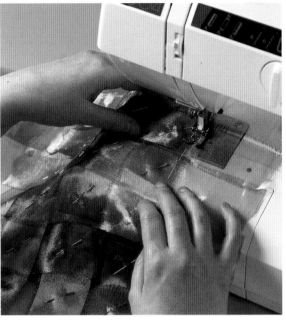

6 Machine-stitch right around the edge of the woven area.

7 Trim the sides and lower edge of the woven area back to 2.5cm/1in.

8 Thread the wooden dowel through the loops along the top. Screw two hooks into the top corners of the window frame to hang the blind.

DRAWN THREADWORK CURTAINS

Square metal "buttons" are the finishing touch on these unusual curtains in which vertical stripes and checks have been created by drawing the threads of the fabric. Instead of a hem at the foot, the curtains are finished with a simple fringe.

YOU WILL NEED
tin snips
small sheet of thin aluminium
drill
sandpaper
scissors
hessian
tape measure
bodkin
iron
pins
sewing machine
matching thread

1 Using tin snips, cut the aluminium into 4cm/1½in squares. You will need about 30 for each curtain, depending on the width of your window. Using a drill, make four holes in the centre of each "button".

2 Rub each button on a piece of sandpaper to smooth the sharp corners.

3 Cut the hessian (burlap) to size, allowing a 2cm/¾in seam allowance at the upper edge. Using a bodkin, draw out threads in vertical stripes at 20cm/8in intervals across the curtains. Draw out about nine threads, leave four then draw out another nine. Reserve the drawn threads.

68

4 Draw out two parallel horizontal bands in the same way, about 20cm/8in and 40cm/16in above the hemline.

5 Fray the lower edge of the curtains to a depth of about 4cm/1½in.

6 Using the bodkin and the drawn threads, sew a button to the centre of each drawn-out intersection with a cross stitch.

7 Calculate the number of tabs you will need for each curtain, placing one above each stripe and one at each end. Cut a rectangle of fabric for each tab, using the template at the back of the book. Fold each rectangle in half lengthways, press and stitch, with a 1cm/½in seam allowance.

8 Open out the seam allowance and pin and stitch across one end of each tab so the seam lies at the centre. Turn to the right side and press.

▶

9 Pin the raw ends of the tabs to the right side of each curtain, corresponding with the vertical stripes. Fold and stitch a 2cm/¾in hem down each side. (If possible, use the selvedge to reduce bulk.)

10 For the facing, cut a 10cm/4in strip of fabric the width of the curtain plus 4cm/1½in for seam allowances. Pin the strip to the curtain with right sides together and machine stitch the top edge.

11 Fold the facing to the wrong side, fold in the seam allowances at each end and along the raw edge and pin in place.

12 Machine stitch close to the folded edge. Fold the tabs over on to the front and hand stitch a button to hold each one in place.

CHIFFON DRAPES

Lengths of chiffon in jewel colours make a pretty and very easy window decoration.
Use the full width of the fabric so that the selvedges form the side hems. For a wider window,
just thread extra lengths on to the wires.

YOU WILL NEED
tape measure
scissors
chiffon in main and second colour
iron
sewing machine
matching thread
wire cutters
plastic-coated curtain wire
4 screw-in eyes
2 or 4 screw-in hooks
silk cord

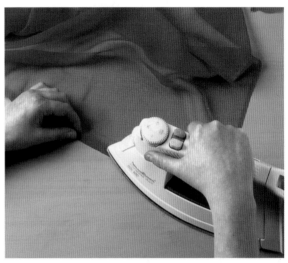

1 Measure the window and cut two corresponding lengths of chiffon in the main colour and one in the second colour. Fold over and press 1cm/½in along the top edge of each piece.

2 Fold over a further 2.5cm/1in on each top edge.

3 Machine-stitch close to the first fold to form a casing for the curtain wire.

4 Cut two lengths of curtain wire 2.5cm/1in shorter than the width of the window. Attach screw-in eyes to the ends.

▶

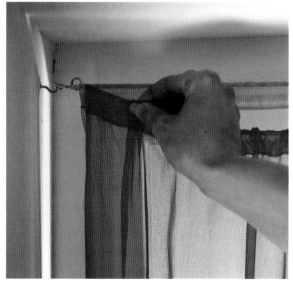

5 Thread one curtain wire through the two curtains in the main colour, and the other through the second colour curtain.

6 Screw hooks into place in the top corners of the window. Hook the curtain wires on to the hooks so that the single curtain hangs behind the pair.

7 Gather the bottom of each main colour curtain to one side of the window and tie it with a 1m/1yd length of silk cord.

8 Criss-cross the cords around the curtains, tucking the raw ends into the bundles. Double knot the cords and trim off the excess. (If you wish, you can loop each cord over a hook screwed into the side of the window frame.) Repeat with the second colour curtain, but gather it in the centre of the window.

GLITTERING BEAD CURTAIN

Much prettier than net curtains, multicoloured beads will dress your window without obscuring the view. Nylon line supports the beads invisibly, and large beads at the end of each pendant give weight and add definition to the shape.

YOU WILL NEED
pencil
ruler
4cm/1¹/₂in wide wooden batten to fit window
drill
scissors
nylon fishing line
selection of plastic beads, including large drops and long or
bugle beads, in various colours and sizes
large pendant beads
4cm/1¹/₂in wide ribbon
staple gun
2 screw-in hooks

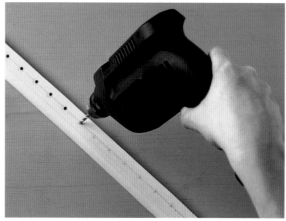

1 Using a pencil and ruler, mark points 2.5cm/1in apart all along the wooden batten, 2.5cm/1in from one edge. Allow enough space between the first and second holes at each end for the window frame. Drill a hole at each point.

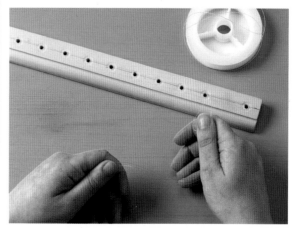

2 Cut a length of fishing line twice the length of the window plus 50cm/20in. Thread both ends through the second hole, then through the loop. ▶

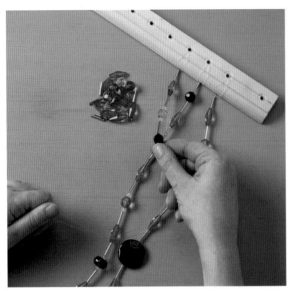

3 Pull the fishing line taut. Thread on the beads in
a random manner, using bugle or long beads to
space out the round beads.

4 When you reach the desired length, thread on
a large pendant bead, pass the fishing line back
through the last few beads and make a knot. Thread
the fishing line back up the length of the strand,
knotting the ends twice more, and trim the ends.

5 Repeat the process for the other strands, making
them shorter towards the centre of the window.
Cut a length of ribbon to the length of the batten
plus 2cm/¾in. Staple it in position at either end.
Attach a screw-in hook at either end of the batten
to hang the curtain.

RIBBON-TIED BLIND

The simplest of all blinds to construct, this straightforward design can be raised to any height by knotting its ribbon ties. The lower edge is held straight by a length of dowel – roll the blind up around it or just push it up in informal gathers.

YOU WILL NEED
scissors
two co-ordinating fabrics for blind and lining
pins
sewing machine
matching thread
iron
saw
9mm/⅜in wooden dowel
needle
petersham ribbon
touch-and-close fasteners
wooden batten to fit window

1 Cut the two fabrics to fit the window, adding 4cm/1½in to the width and 9cm/3½in to the length. Pin the pieces right sides together and machine-stitch the side and bottom seams, leaving the top edge open. Trim the corners and turn through to the right side. Press.

2 Cut a piece of dowel to the width of the blind. Fit it into the bottom of the blind.

3 Slip-stitch the top edge and press the seam.

4 Top-stitch 5cm/2in from the side edges and 2cm/¾in from the top and bottom edges.

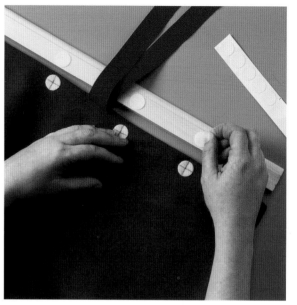

5 Cut four pieces of petersham ribbon to the length of the blind plus 20cm/8in. Pin two pairs of ties, one on the right side and one on the wrong side of the blind, about a quarter of the width in from the side.

6 Machine-stitch the ties in place at the top edge. Stitch the soft side of the touch-and-close fasteners to the wrong side along the top. Stick the hooked side of the touch-and-close fasteners to the front of the batten.

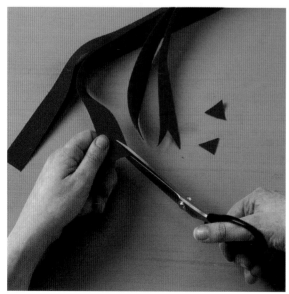

7 Trim the ends of the ribbons with scissors to make decorative points.

8 Knot each pair of ribbons at the required height, allowing the ribbon ends to hang down.

STRIKING CONTRAST

In most window treatments the lining is unobtrusive, but here it becomes the focal point. The contrasting colours of these silks make a forceful statement, but a plain fabric with a patterned lining would also look effective.

YOU WILL NEED
tape measure
scissors
silk fabric
contrasting silk lining fabric
heavyweight interfacing
sewing machine
matching thread
iron
pins
needle
fabric marker or tailor's chalk
eyelet kit
hammer
15mm/⅝in brass eyelets
2.5cm/1in wide satin ribbon

1 Measure the window and cut two pieces of each fabric and two pieces of interfacing to the finished size plus 2cm/¾in seam allowance all round. Cut two 20 x 6cm/8 x 2½in strips of lining fabric. Fold lengthways, right sides together, and stitch the long edge leaving a 1cm/½in seam allowance. Trim the seam, turn through and press.

2 Fold each strip in half widthways to make a loop. Pin the two raw edges of each loop to the lower inside corner of the right side of each lining piece.

3 Place the fabric and lining right sides together, then lay the interfacing on top. Pin and stitch the edges, catching in the ends of each loop at the lower corner, and leaving a gap of 40cm/16in in the top edge. Turn to the right side and slip-stitch the gap. ▶

4 At even intervals across the top edge, mark the positions of the
  eyelets with a fabric marker or tailor's chalk, placing one near
each corner.

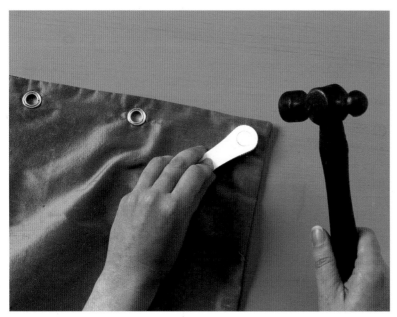

5 Using an eyelet tool and a hammer, insert the eyelets across the top
  edge. Cut a length of ribbon for each eyelet hole, thread it through
and knot firmly to the curtain pole.

MATERIALS

Part of the pleasure of making your own curtains and blinds is using everyday materials, such as buttons and beads, hooks and eyes, to create varied and delightful effects.

BOBBLE TRIM
A decorative woven trim with small pompoms, to stitch or glue to the edge of a curtain or blind.

BUTTONS
Use buttons as decorative details on tab-headed curtains.

CORD
Fine nylon cord is used to draw up Roman blinds into pleats.

CURTAIN HOOKS AND RINGS
These are available in a variety of different sizes, weights and designs.

CURTAIN RODS AND WIRE
Tension rods and screw-in net rods are used for small or recessed windows. Plastic-covered wire is used for fine curtains.

DOUBLE-SIDED TAPE
Used to fold up hems on paper blinds and to attach lightweight blinds to battens.

DOWEL
Narrow wooden dowel rods are used when making Roman blinds, passed through horizontal channels.

EYELETS AND EYELET KIT
Metal eyelets are available in various sizes.

FABRIC PAINT
This specialist paint is permanent and washable when dry.

FABRIC STIFFENER
Spray fabric stiffener adds body to fine fabric when making roller blinds or window panels.

FUSIBLE BONDING WEB
Fine adhesive fabric on a paper backing, used with a hot iron to bond fabrics together.

HEADING TAPES
A wide variety of heading tapes are available from most craft shops.

INTERFACING
Used for stiffening fabric, iron-on interfacing has an adhesive backing to iron on to the wrong side of fabric. Choose from a variety of weights.

LATH
Thin stripwood is inserted in a casing at the bottom of a blind to keep it straight and add weight.

PLASTIC BEADS
Plastic beads can be threaded on fishing line to make bead curtains, or stitched on as decoration. Heavier beads are used to weight lightweight curtains or panels.

RIBBONS
Used for ties and decoration or stitched together to make panels for small windows.

SCREW-IN HOOKS AND EYES
Hooks screwed at the top of the window frame support a light-weight blind. Screw-in eyes are used in the end of curtain wires, and under battens to take the cords for raising blinds.

SEWING THREAD
Polyester thread is suitable for machine sewing. Use cotton and silk thread with special fabrics.

TOUCH-AND-CLOSE FASTENERS
Used to fix blinds or pelmets to battens, touch-and-close strips and patches may be self-adhesive or sewing quality or a combination of both.

Opposite: curtain rings (1); double-sided tape (2); fabric stiffener (3); ribbons (4); heading tapes (5); cord (6); bobble trim (7); interfacing (8); fusible bonding web (9); eyelets and eyelet kit (10); tension rod (11); dowel (12); lath (13); fabric paint (14); sewing thread (15); buttons (16); touch-and-close fasteners (17); screw-in hooks (18); plastic-covered wire (19); curtain hooks (20); plastic beads (21); tassle (22).

EQUIPMENT

*The equipment needed for making curtains and blinds is easily available and
probably already in your sewing kit or toolbox.*

ACETATE SHEET
Stencils cut from acetate are
durable and easy to position.

DRILL
An electric drill is needed for
drilling holes in wooden battens
and window frames.

HAMMER
Use a small hammer with eyelet
kits and for tacking blinds to battens.

IRON
A good iron gives a professional
finish.

NEEDLES
You will need sewing needles in
various sizes for tacking, hand
stitching and embroidery. Use a
large bodkin for thick threads.

PATTERN PAPER
Use squared pattern paper for
enlarging designs.

PENCILS
Use soft pencils for tracing
templates and marking battens.

PINS
Rustless steel pins are used for
holding pieces of fabric in place
while tacking or machine stitching, and as temporary markers.

RULER
For drawing straight lines and
checking seam allowances.

SANDPAPER
Use to smooth surfaces of wooden
battens or poles. Sanding produces
a fine dust, so wear a mask.

SAW
Use a small hacksaw for trimming
wooden battens and dowel to size.

SCISSORS
Use a large pair for cutting out
fabric, a smaller all-purpose pair
for paper patterns and cords, and a
small pair for fine work.

SET SQUARE
It is essential to cut fabric straight.
Place the set square against the
selvedge and mark a line across
the width from which to measure
subsequent curtain lengths.

SEWING MACHINE
Even if you hand-sew hems, you
will need a sewing machine for
headings and seams. Straight and
zig-zag stitch are essential for basic
construction.

SPIRIT LEVEL
To make sure that pelmets, poles
and battens are level.

SPONGE
For decorative paint effects and for
use with stencils.

STAMPS
Ready-made stamps can be used
with fabric paints.

STAPLE GUN
Invaluable for quickly and securely
fixing blinds to battens.

STENCIL BRUSH
A large round brush for use with
stencils.

TAILOR'S CHALK
Makes temporary marks on fabric
which can be brushed away later.

TAPE MEASURES
It is worthwhile to have both a
flexible and a retractable steel tape.

TRACING PAPER
Use to trace templates and to
transfer designs to fabric or paper.

*Opposite: stamps (1); spirit level (2); ruler
(3); set square (4); pattern paper (5);
sandpaper (6); sewing machine (7); iron
(8); pencils (9); acetate sheet (10); saw
(11); staple gun (12); drill (13); tape
measure (14); hammer (15); sponge (16);
stencil brush (17); scissors (18); needles
(19); pins (20); tailor's chalk (21).*

MEASURING UP

*The first and most important task when making your own blinds and curtains is
to measure and cut out the fabric accurately.*

MEASURING THE WINDOW
You need to take two basic
measurements to enable you to
estimate the amount of fabric
needed for curtains or blinds.

1 Width
For curtains, measure the width of
the track or pole.

For blinds, measure the width of
the window or recess in which the
blind is to fit.

2 Length
For curtains, the length is a matter
of personal choice: measure from
the top of the track or pole, and
decide whether the curtains are to
fall to the floor, the windowsill or,
for example, the top of a radiator.

For blinds, measure the length
of the window or recess.

CALCULATING THE AMOUNT OF
FABRIC FOR CURTAINS
Generally, the total width of a
curtain should be at least 1½–2
times the width of the track or
pole for standard tapes, and more
for others. Tape manufacturers
usually recommend the fullness you
will need to achieve the desired
pleating effect with any heading.

1 To calculate the number of widths
Multiply the width of the track or
pole by the fabric fullness required
for the tape you are using. Add
about 10cm/4in for each curtain
for seams and side hems. Divide
the total by the width of your
chosen fabric to give the number
of fabric widths required, round-
ing up to the nearest full number.

2 To calculate the total fabric length
Take the curtain length from track
or pole to hem, then add about
20cm/8in for the hem and heading. Multiply this figure by the
number of fabric widths required.
If the fabric has a repeat pattern,
add on the length of one full
repeat for each fabric width.

If the fabric is washable it may
shrink. Allow an extra 10cm/4in
per metre/yard for shrinkage and
launder the fabric before cutting
out the curtains.

CALCULATING THE AMOUNT OF
FABRIC FOR BLINDS
In general, the fabric requirement
for blinds is given by the window
or recess measurement from top to
bottom plus seam allowances
down either side and at the lower
edge. You should allow about
5cm/2in at the top for attachment
to the batten.

CUTTING OUT THE FABRIC
Always lay the fabric out on a
large flat table or the floor. Begin
with a straight edge: to do this
draw out a weft (horizontal)
thread from the width of the
fabric, then use this line as a
guide for cutting. Measure the
first fabric piece from this edge.

If the fabric is patterned, you
must match the pattern repeats on
each piece cut. It is usually easiest
to cut the first piece, then lay it
on the rest of the fabric and use it
as a guide for subsequent pieces.

BASIC TECHNIQUES

Curtains and blinds should fit your needs perfectly. Experiment with the wide variety of heading tapes and decorative hooks and clips now available to achieve individual results every time.

PENCIL PLEAT

Fabric fullness required: 2–2½ times track/pole measurement. A popular heading resulting in tall regular pleats across the curtain, available in various depths and also in a lightweight version.

STANDARD

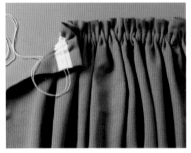

Fabric fullness required: 1½ times track/pole measurement. A simple gathered effect which works most successfully on lightweight or unlined curtains.

BOX PLEAT

Fabric fullness required: twice track/pole measurement. By drawing up the cords the curtain forms flat box pleats at regular intervals across the width.

TRIPLE PINCH PLEAT

Fabric fullness required: twice track/pole measurement. By pulling the two draw cords, the fabric will be gathered into evenly spaced elegant pinch pleats. Take care to ensure that the pleating positions match on both curtains. It is available in various depths and also in a lightweight version.

NET/VOILE PLEAT

Fabric fullness required: twice track/pole measurement. A translucent heading tape for use with sheer voile fabrics or nets. In addition to the pockets in the tape to take curtain hooks, there are loops enabling the curtain to be suspended from a rod or wire.

GOBLET

Fabric fullness required: 2½ times track/pole measurement. The top cord draws the fabric into rounded pleats across the width, while the lower cord gathers the base of each to form goblet shapes. These shapes can be further enhanced by stuffing lightly with tissue paper, which holds the rounded shape.

HEADING VARIATIONS

TIES

As an alternative to a plain tab top, stitch two long tabs in pairs along the curtain top, then tie in decorative bows or knots.

EYELETS AND HOOKS

Use decorative hooks to attach a curtain to a narrow pole. Insert eyelets at approximately 15cm/6in intervals across a double hem at the top of the curtain.

DECORATIVE CLIPS

There are many decorative clips available to choose from, ideal for hanging lightweight curtains or panels without the need for stitched-on tapes. Simply clip on to the curtain and then slip on to a pole or curtain rod.

SMALL CLIPS

Small decorative clips are available for use with lightweight or sheer curtains and a pole or rod. They are ideally suited to a small window or a café-style curtain.

TENSION ROD

A tension rod is used for lightweight or café curtains in a recessed window where it is difficult to fit a track or pole. The rod is slipped through a stitched casing at the top of the curtain.

CURTAIN WIRE

Used for lightweight voiles or nets, the plastic-coated wire is trimmed to size then passed through a casing at the top of the fabric. A metal hook can then be inserted into each end ready to hook on to metal eyes screwed into the window frame.

BASIC TAB HEADING

1 Cut out a rectangle of fabric for each tab, following the template at the back of the book. Fold in half lengthways, with right sides together. Stitch together along the long edge with a 1cm/½in seam allowance.

2 For tab curtains with button fastenings or decorations, open the seam with your fingers at one end of the tab and pin together so the seam lies at the centre of the tab. Stitch across the end with a 1cm/½in seam allowance.

3 Trim the seam allowance and snip across the corners to reduce bulk. Turn the tab through to the right side and press. Turn the tab in half widthways.

4 Pin the tabs to the right side of the curtain, matching the raw edges of the tabs to the top edge of the curtain. Lay a facing strip on top with right sides together and stitch along the top edge with a 2cm/¾in seam allowance. Fold the facing to the wrong side of the curtain and press, then fold in the seam allowance along the raw edge and stitch in place. Tuck in the raw edges at each end and slip-stitch.

INSERTING EYELETS

1 First mark the eyelet positions with a pencil, spacing them evenly. Place the plastic disc underneath the fabric at the first mark, then place the cutting part of the eyelet tool over the mark and strike with a hammer to punch the hole.

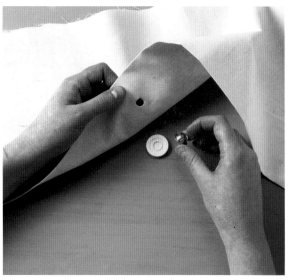

2 Turn the disc over and place the eyelet on it. Bring the fabric down so that the punched hole fits over the eyelet.

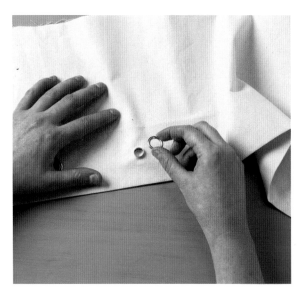

3 Place the washer over the eyelet.

4 Place the flanging part of the tool over the washer and hammer to complete the eyelet.

SEAMS AND HEMS

PLAIN SEAM

A simple seam suitable for joining most fabrics.

1 Pin, tack and machine-stitch the two pieces of fabric with right sides together, with a 2cm/¾in seam allowance. If the fabric has a pattern, be sure it matches.

2 Remove the tacking and press the seam open. To prevent puckering at the selvedge, use sharp scissors to clip the seam allowance at 10cm/4in intervals.

FRENCH SEAM

This quick and neat seam is perfect for using with sheer or fine fabrics where a plain seam would be unsightly.

1 Pin, tack and machine-stitch the fabric, keeping the wrong sides together, with a 1cm/½in seam allowance. Trim the seam allowance a little.

2 Press the seam open then refold, this time with right sides together. Pin, tack and machine-stitch 1cm/½in from the first seam line, enclosing all raw edges.

NO-SEW SEAM

For fine and lightweight fabrics use a fusible adhesive bonding strip to make a no-sew hem.

1 Measure, fold and press the hem then place the bonding strip between the hem and the fabric. Use a hot iron to press the hem so that the adhesive melts and fuses the layers of fabric together.

TEMPLATES

Enlarge the templates on a photocopier. Alternatively, trace the design and draw a grid of evenly spaced squares over your tracing. Draw a larger grid on to another piece of paper and copy the outline square by square. Draw over the lines to make sure they are continuous.

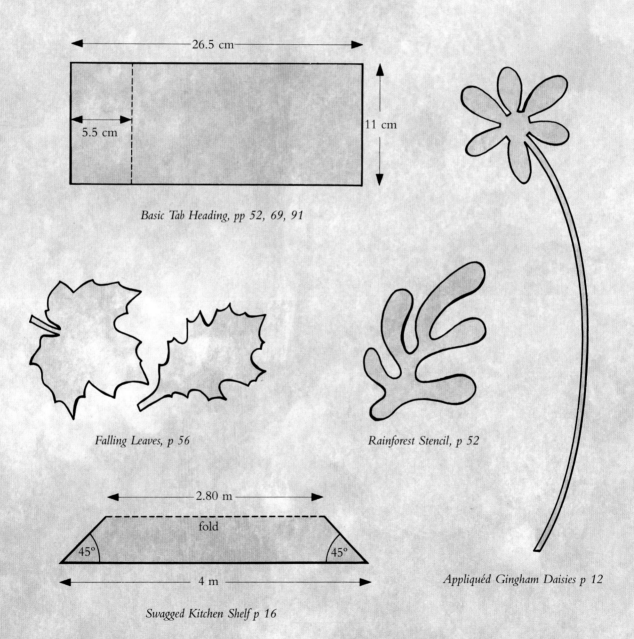

Basic Tab Heading, pp 52, 69, 91

Falling Leaves, p 56

Rainforest Stencil, p 52

Swagged Kitchen Shelf p 16

Appliquéd Gingham Daisies p 12

SUPPLIERS

Much of the material needed for these projects can be found in most large department stores. Look in your local telephone directory for the nearest stores.

UK
Ellis & Farrier
20 Beak Street
London W1R 3HA
Beads, sequins

John Lewis Plc
Oxford Street
London W1A 1EX
Fabrics, furnishing fabrics, trimmings, ribbons, beads, curtain tapes

Nu-Line
315 Westbourne Park Road
London W11
General hardware, sheet metal suppliers

Paperchase
Tottenham Court Road
London W1
Paper specialists, paints and artist's materials

Russell & Chapple
23 Monmouth Street
London WC2H 9DE
Canvas, calico suppliers

Woolfin Textiles & Co
64 Great Titchfield Street
London W1
Range of natural fabrics, calico, hessian (burlap)

USA
Britex Fabrics
146 Geary Street
San Francisco, CA 94108
Fabrics, wide range of general craft materials and equipment

Dick Blick
P.O. Box 1267
Galesburg, IL 61402
Wide range of general craft items

Pearl Paint
Canal Street
New York, NY 10011
Paint specialists, general craft items

ACKNOWLEDGEMENTS

The publishers would like to thank the following people for designing the projects in this book: Petra Boase for the Kitchen Print Curtains pp24–27, Ribbon Flowers pp42–44, Voile Stripes pp45–47; Rachel Frost for the Swagged Kitchen Shelf pp16–19, Stamped Calico Blind pp34–37, Slatted Brocade Blind pp59–61, Double Fan Blind pp62–64, Woven Organza Blind pp65–67, Chiffon Drapes pp72–74; Alison Jenkins for the Basic Lined Curtains pp8–11, Ribbon Café Curtain pp31–33, Orchard Print Curtains and Blind pp38–41, Pleated Tissue Blind pp48–51, Rainforest Stencil pp52–55, Falling Leaves pp56–58, Drawn Threadwork Curtains pp68–71; Isabel Stanley for the Appliquéd Gingham Daisies pp12–15, Cut-out Denim Roller Blind pp20–23, Draped Muslin Curtains pp28–30, Glittering Bead Curtain pp75–77, Ribbon-tied Blind pp78–80, Striking Contrast pp81–83.

INDEX